Do Breathe

Calm your mind.
Find focus.
Get stuff done.

Michael Townsend Williams

CHRONICLE BOOKS
SAN FRANCISCO

First published in the United States of America in 2018 by Chronicle Books LLC.
First published in the United Kingdom in 2015 by The Do Book Company.

Text copyright © 2015 by Michael Townsend Williams.
Photography copyright © 2015 by Jonathan Cherry.
Photography p36, 58, 90 copyright © 2015 by Mickey Smith.
Photography p21 copyright © 2015 by Wilf Whitty.
Lettering p3, 44, 119 copyright © 2015 by James Victore.

Library of Congress Cataloging-in-Publication Data

Names: Williams, Michael Townsend, author.
Title: Do breathe / Michael Townsend Williams.
Description: San Francisco, California : Chronicle Books LLC, 2018. |
  Originally published in United Kingdom in 2015 by The Do Book Company. |
  Includes index.
Identifiers: LCCN 2018000250 | ISBN 9781452171692 (pbk. : alk. paper)
Subjects: LCSH: Breathing exercises. | Meditation--Therapeutic use. | Mind
  and body therapies.
Classification: LCC RA782 .W55 2018 | DDC 613/.192--dc23 LC record available at
https://lccn.loc.gov/2018000250

Manufactured in China.

Cover design by James Victore.
Book designed and set by Ratiotype.

10 9 8 7 6 5 4 3 2 1

Chronicle Books LLC
680 Second Street
San Francisco, California 94107
www.chroniclebooks.com

For Jonathan

Breathe in...

Contents

Introduction

As I danced to the sound of The Police's "Every Breath You Take" in a bar in Kuala Lumpur, tears ran down my face. My thirty-one-year-old brother Jonathan had accidentally fallen from the balcony of his fifteenth floor apartment and died on impact. A day later I was there to sort out his affairs with my cousin Nigel. We spent the night with Jonathan's friends and colleagues in a daze of despair and disorientation. Little did I know this tragic event would send my life on such a different trajectory.

Until then I'd worked in advertising. I wasn't a flashy adman. More of a drunk one. A production guy who got things done while managing an alcohol addiction that imperfectly masked a life out of control. When shit happens we wake up. Life is short. I realized I hated the rut I was in and wanted out. But how?

I had no idea what I wanted to do. Addiction drives out hobbies and interests until the only thing left is the addiction and maybe, if you're lucky, a long-suffering partner. As I sobered up—both literally and from the grieving process—one love rose to the surface. Yoga. It had always been my way of handling stress and depression and had become a place of refuge.

When, unexpectedly, I stepped into the role of a teacher on a family holiday at Monkton Wyld Court, a community near Lyme Regis in Dorset, I lit a candle, an incense stick, and a place inside my heart. I had found my calling—or had my calling found me?

Since 2002 I have continued to teach yoga in places like the National Portrait Gallery, the National Gallery, and Tate Britain, as well as classes locally.

I have run workshops and retreats. And from my love of yoga came my awareness of the power of breathing.

Awareness of our breath connects us to the way we move, the way we think, and the way we feel. The way we breathe reflects the way we live. Animals that breathe quickly die early. Animals that breathe slowly live longer. And we could all slow down a bit more, couldn't we?

> "If I had to limit my advice on healthier living to just one tip, it would be simply to learn how to breathe correctly."
>
> —
>
> Dr. Andrew Weil

Everything that exists has a rhythm. From the light pulsing from distant planets to the beating of our hearts, everything in nature is connected.

Our breath is perhaps the greatest connector of all. It connects us to our planet. When we breathe out, plants breathe in. Our breath connects our bodies with our minds—when we slow down, we think better.

> "Breathing creates the platform on which everything else—health, happiness, cognitive ability, and elevated performance, success, and influence—is built."

> Dr Alan Watkins

Do Breathe is divided into three parts. The first part, Prepare, is designed to prepare you both mentally and physically with the foundations for a better life. It is subdivided into three chapters: "Breathe," "Organize," and "Courage."

The second part, "Practice," will get your mind and body moving in practical ways that will support you moment by moment, day by day. Within this section I discuss Mindfulness, Energy, and Focus.

Finally, Part 3: "Perform." This section of three chapters—"Flow," "Habits," and "Well-Doing"—will help you manage the ups and downs of your life better and create meaningful change.

So, are you ready to breathe yourself better?

PREPARE

1
Breathe

When you arise in the morning
think what a precious privilege
it is to be alive: to breathe,
to think, to enjoy, to love.

Marcus Aurelius

**The Roman emperor Marcus Aurelius wrote this
while on the battlefield around AD 170. He believed
a clear mind allowed us to live in harmony with
"logos"—a sense of universal order. For some ancient
philosophers, this harmony was divine, for others, a
principle of order and knowledge. Either way I find it
amusing that the word "logo," which was part of my
everyday life in advertising for many years, has its
origins in philosophy and self-inquiry.**

In our lives we find harmony, order, and a clear mind
all too elusive. On today's commercial battlefields the
enemies are more self-inflicted: stress, pressure, lack
of sleep, an unhealthy diet, too much alcohol, too little
rest . . . you know the score.

So when you arise in the morning you probably feel
tired and irritable, and the last thing on your mind is
breathing and actually enjoying your life. Wouldn't it be
refreshing if that were different?

Why Breathing?

From our first to our last breath, we breathe in and out somewhere in the region of six hundred million times. We take it for granted. It just happens, doesn't it? What's the big deal? We breathe in oxygen and we breathe out carbon dioxide. As my son said: "How are you going to write a whole book about that, Dad?" However, there's a lot more to the breath than that.

Breath is the crucial link between the mind and the body. It's the only system in the body that works both consciously and unconsciously. It affects how all our other internal systems work (digestion, the immune system, heart, nerves, brain, etc.). It both reflects and influences whatever is going on at any given moment in our minds and bodies. Our breath is also our only constant companion on life's journey. Isn't it worth knowing how to breathe better, then?

Let's start by looking at two important coping mechanisms that have evolved in the human body to help us deal with life's challenges.

The Stress Response

Our bodies are designed to maintain balance. The medical term is homeostasis. So our bodies are always looking to maintain the right temperature, the right amount of oxygen and carbon dioxide, the right level of acidity and alkalinity, the right amount of sleep, etc. Threats to this balance are called stressors—such as like being attacked by an animal or starving through lack of food. Our built-in fight-or-flight response releases adrenaline and myriad other hormones to get us out of trouble. It evolved as a quick fix for extreme circumstances. However, our bodies are simply not designed to experience it too often. Yet nowadays, even the most mundane crisis like missing a train can trigger fight, flight, or even a third possibility, freeze. We are chronically overreacting, and we are paying the price—heart disease, depression, and obesity as well as wrecked jobs and ruined relationships. The World Health Organization has called stress "the health epidemic of the twenty-first century."

The Relaxation Response

Controlled deep breathing has been shown to produce the body's "relaxation response." As with the stress response, a number of hormones are released in the body; however, these hormones slow down our heart rate, relax muscles, calm our nerves, and improve our immune system. It also creates the ideal conditions for digesting food well. And yet how often do we make stress worse by gobbling down a sandwich at our desks, causing indigestion and putting more pressure on our bodies?

Both of these responses work two ways: Being stressed or relaxed affects how you breathe, and your breathing dictates how stressed or relaxed you feel. With better awareness of your breath, you can more easily notice early signs of stress (shallow or faster breathing) and induce the relaxation response to stop it from getting worse.

"In as little as one minute of focused breathing it's possible to completely clear the bloodstream of the stress hormone cortisol."

Tony Schwartz, *Harvard Business Review* (2012)

The "Bodymind"

You may have noticed by now that sometimes I'm referring to the effects of breathing, stress, and relaxation on the mind and sometimes on the body. In fact there is only one "bodymind." Your body affects your mind and your mind affects your body. All too often, however, we listen to the neurotic ramblings of our mind and ignore the pleas of our bodies: "Please rest, please move, please eat . . ." Once we start to listen and pay attention to our minds, our bodies, and our breathing, we can really start to build strong foundations for a better day, and a better life.

Breathe like a Baby

Do you have a child? Do you remember watching them sleep as babies, their bellies naturally rising and falling? Do you remember their first breath? When I did a talk recently, I introduced my breathing guru by showing a photo of a baby—because babies are the best breathers. Their minds and bodies are one. They breathe well because as human beings they are designed to. We can learn from them. Breathe from the belly, breathe through the nose. It's as simple as that. Who knows, it might also help you sleep like a baby.

How Are You Breathing Now?

If breathing well is so natural, why do we lose the knack? When was the last time you stopped and noticed how you were breathing? Have you made the connection already between your breathing and how you feel? How about now? What do you observe? Are you breathing through your nose or your mouth? Can you feel your belly rising and falling? Or can you feel your chest lifting and expanding? Maybe you're even holding your breath?

The first step to improving how you breathe is awareness. Start to become more and more aware of how you breathe and how that changes under different conditions. Don't just follow this book, follow your own breath—it's your best teacher.

The Three Keys to Breathing Well

There are many breathing exercises and techniques from both the East and the West. You will find a number of them throughout the book. The basics, however, are simple.

1. **Breathe in and out from the belly.**
   When you breathe from the belly, you feel more centered and more in control. This diaphragmatic or abdominal breathing (I prefer to say "belly") is efficient and, once established, easy and natural.

2. **Breathe in and out through the nose.**
   The nose is designed for breathing. The little hairs in the nostrils filter out particles in the air. The chamber behind the nose cools or warms the air to within one degree of the body's temperature. Except for certain situations like high-intensity sports, your nose does a much better job of breathing than your mouth.

3. **Breathe out a little more than you breathe in.**
   Exhaling is linked to the body's relaxation response, as it stimulates the parasympathetic branch of the autonomic nervous system. Once you're in balance, you can breathe in and out equally. But in my experience most of us are so frequently stressed that a little more exhalation with every breath is a good idea.

The Benefits

As well as reducing stress and relaxing us more, breathing well has a number of other benefits. In research, controlled breathing has been shown to lower blood pressure and heart rate. According to the World Health Organization, cardiovascular disease is the number one cause of death in the world, so maybe it's time for you to look after your heart with your breath. There is also evidence that breathing well can improve our brains. After regular breathing practice, the brain grows in areas that are linked to attention and the processing of sensory information. By reducing the stress response, you also engage the prefrontal cortex, which is where your brain makes decisions—breathing helps you think better.

There is also even more amazing research showing that breathing well affects how your genes express themselves. Herbert Benson, who first coined the phrase *relaxation response* in his book of the same name, was involved in research in 2008 showing that genes influencing how we respond to stress are altered through relaxed breathing techniques. So the next time you breathe, remember how it helps your heart, your brain, and your genes, as well as how you feel. And that's not all, as you will find out as you make your way through the book.

Exercise to Breathe Better Now

— Lie down on your back in a room that is relatively quiet.
  Close the door, and put your phone in airplane mode.
— If you find it uncomfortable, raise your knees with your feet
  on the floor. This will give your lower back better support.
— Place a hardback book on your belly.
— Now try to breathe in and out through the nose, making the
  book rise and fall with your belly. If your chest continues to
  move as you breathe, place a hand on your chest and press
  down firmly to encourage you to use the belly more.
— So as you breathe in, the belly rises. As you breathe out,
  the belly falls (draw your belly down toward the floor).
  Breathe in and out through the nose. Once you are getting
  into the rhythm, start to lengthen your exhalation. Count to
  three as you breathe in and count to six as you breathe out.
  If you find that hard, just do the best you can.
— Lie there for at least five minutes. You can set a timer on
  your phone.

Things to Remember

1. Breathe in and out from the belly.
2. Breathe in and out through the nose.
3. Breathe out a bit more than you breathe in.

Rather than just sleep like a baby, breathe like a baby,
and you will not only sleep better, but also feel better
and focus more.

Meet your breathing guru

2
Organize

> Anxiety is caused by a lack of control,
> organization, preparation, and action.
>
> ---
>
> David Kekich

Linda Stone, the writer, speaker, and consultant, coined the term *email apnoea* when she discovered that workers were so stressed by their email inboxes that at times they held their breath. Shallow or intermittent breathing, feeling anxious, and lacking energy are all signs that perhaps you are holding too much information in your head.

We all like to think that the stress and anxiety in our lives is due to outside influences. Sometimes the whole world appears to conspire against us. The causes can be money, or the lack of it, our jobs, our partners, our children . . . the weather, the train, traffic . . . our declining health, our computers, our phones . . . you get the idea. To paraphrase Jean-Paul Sartre, "Stress is other people!"

However true this may appear to be, we don't exactly help ourselves. We hop from task to task. We say yes when we mean to say no. We can't find things when we need them. We forget appointments. We use our email inbox as our to-do list. We use our email inbox as our filing system. We can't stop checking Facebook, Twitter, Instagram, Pinterest, Medium, Tumblr, Google+ . . . OK, maybe not all of them. We get buzzes and beeps from our phones, our computers, our ovens, and our dishwashers. Life itself seems to be out of control. Although the truth is you are the one out of control.

One of the most powerful motivators for me was the clarity and peace of mind that comes from being better organized. Our minds are not designed to hold the amount of information that we expect them to cope with. Neuroscientists refer to our ability to hold stuff in our working memory as cognitive load. When we overdo it, we get information overload—we can't think clearly, we make poor decisions, we feel stressed, and the quality of our breathing drops. The best way to address this is by performing a mind sweep and getting everything out of your head, and there is an exercise at the end of this chapter to help you do this.

"But creative people thrive on chaos!" I hear you say. "Organization is for boring people." "I haven't got time to get organized." "One day I will earn enough so I can pay someone else to do all this stuff."

I know where you're coming from. I, too, held these beliefs until one day I got so fed up with living in a state of stress, anxiety, and not getting stuff done, I decided to learn how to get organized.

The Art of Doing

No one teaches us the art of doing. We are thrown in the deep end at school, somehow avoid drowning in college, and end up splashing wildly through our working lives. The emphasis is on results, not on how you get there. The solutions to our chaos are sold to us in the form of books, apps, filing systems, and beautifully designed stationery and bespoke pens and pencils. And we consume them avidly. Alas, they offer only temporary respite. Because the only solution to us being disorganized is getting organized!

So if you are reluctantly accepting that it's you who might need to change, you are on the right track. And it's not only about doing more; by learning the art of doing, you will also discover the art of being. This chapter will take you through a simplified approach that I have implemented personally and coached many others in. It is not a complete guide but will give you enough to get started. There are further resources at the end of the book.

CARE about What You Do

The simple framework that I use myself and with my coaching clients is to C-A-R-E about what they do:

Collect   **Arrange**   **Reflect**   **Execute**

Collect your stuff

At present you probably have two or three email accounts, mail arriving at home and at work, messages on your phone, messages on social media, voicemails on your mobile and your home phone (if you still have one), documents on your desk, scribbles on a notebook (or several), a pad with an important phone number (somewhere), business cards and receipts in your wallet, a draft presentation outline in your laptop case with notes from your last meeting, notes on your phone's notes app, photos of things you think are cool, and oh so many brilliant ideas in your head.

So let's start the process by creating a simpler way of gathering new inputs into your life:

— Get all your email into one inbox
— Have one physical in-tray at home and one at work
— Carry folder for keeping paper documents (I like a zippy mesh folder thing)
— Have one notebook
— Use one app on your phone to collect stuff

Now turn off all notifications—yes, that's right, all of them (OK, we're all allowed one exception). No more badge icons on your phone with 2,000 unread emails, 43 missed calls, 17 Facebook alerts, 62 unread "read later" articles. No more vibrations. No more beeps. No more unnecessary interruptions.

Seize back control. You decide where your attention goes. You are in charge. If people you work with don't like it, tell them that you are doing it so that you can work, create, and think better, and if they have a problem with that, maybe they need to change! Get tough.

Arrange it systematically

It is very common that people on a mission to get organized get good at getting tidy but fail to maintain things. The reason is they don't have a systematic way of going about it. If you follow this simple process with all the inputs in your life, all the time, it becomes a habit. You won't need to remember what to do or even think about it—it becomes your way.

WORKFLOW
PROCESS

- -

INBOX
Do I need to do something?

YES		NO
DO IT 2 mins or less		**TRASH CAN** Or recycle
DELEGATE Waiting for		**FILE** A–Z Reference
DEFER To-Do List Email "Actions" Folder or Calendar		**SOMEDAY** Later

There are two places where I keep track of my "Actions."

1. **My email "Actions" folder**
2. **My to-do lists**

The first one is straightforward. The second one can be but often isn't. Again, the typical problem arises when someone thinks more about finding the right tool or app than how they will use it. As these tools can vary in approach and style, very soon you can become overwhelmed with choice, confused, and sucked into thinking that the tool and not you is the cause or solution to your stress.

So before we look at some tools I have used and recommended, let's look at the keys to creating effective to-do lists.

— **Use verbs!** If you can't start a to-do list with a verb (like *write, email, call, find, look for,* etc.) you probably haven't worked out the "action" yet.

— **Add place or context.** By either creating separate lists or using tags for different places, you will be able to see what is relevant to where you are. Contexts can be actual physical places (at the office, at home, at the store) or the resources you need (computer, Internet, phone).

— **Create mini-projects.** If something needs more than one action, then highlight this. Decide what the outcome looks like and then list the first three actions at most (no need to overplan). This is a great way to get momentum on the little things of life as well as that big project you still haven't started.

Here's an everyday example:

You need to mail a birthday card to a friend, so you write on your to-do list, "Mail birthday card to Dylan." And as the days pass you just don't do it. Why? Because it can't be done. You don't have the card, you don't have a stamp, and you don't have his new address. So this is what it should look like, with the relevant place in parentheses:

Mini-Project: Mail birthday card to Dylan

Actions:
[ ] Email Dylan to get new address (on the Internet)
[ ] Buy birthday card for Dylan (at the store)
[ ] Buy stamps (at the store)
[ ] Write card (at the office)
[ ] Mail birthday card for Dylan (at the mailbox)

This might appear overkill and yet there is no other way to get it done. Knowing where your actions are kept means no more piles on your desk hiding things you might need to do, and as a result no more nagging feelings in the back of your mind. And when you look at a clear list of actions when you're in the midst of a crazy day at work, you'll be pleased to find that clarity of action. With no need to think, you just need to do.

More and more people and organizations are moving toward paper-free filing. And yet, have you ever seen a paper-free office? Technology companies are often the worst offenders. In my experience you will need to have a simple way of filing stuff both digitally and physically.

Reference items can be notes, documents, photos, scribbles, magazine articles, or just mementos. Clearly labeled and organized filing cabinets are unavoidable. Invest in good ones that will grow with you and avoid temporary solutions like boxes, filing folders, and the like that grow into complicated messes, where it's impossible to find anything. This is what I do:

A simple filing system

— **Use one A to Z system for everything**—family, finances, work, projects etc. Avoid vague categories and "Miscellaneous" folders.

— **Name file folders in an obvious way** (e.g., "Insurance-House" or "House-Insurance").

— **Create handy folders on your desk for quick reference** e.g., "Action Support" (for documents needed to do things), "Waiting For" (for things you've delegated or ordered).

If you still end up with piles, then make two piles—an "Action" pile and a "Reference" pile. Even that simple division will make things a little clearer, both in your outside world and in your mind.

Reflect on your workload

Every day look at your calendar, your to-do lists, and your email actions folder *before* you go looking for more work in your inbox. This simple reordering of how you start your day at the computer will put your agenda first. Every week spend at least an hour having a meeting with yourself. Get your physical and email inboxes clear. Run through your commitments—your to-do lists, your projects, your calendar for the next two weeks.

DAILY REVIEW
YOUR MORNING ROUTINE

1 CALENDAR | Schedule
What does your day look like?

2 LISTS | Today
What's already important?

3 EMAIL | Action Folder
Are there any existing emails that need action?

Email Inbox
Only look here after the above so you are aware of all of your present commitments.

WEEKLY REVIEW
YOUR MOST IMPORTANT MEETING

1 CLEAR THE DECKS
Process all inboxes to zero.

2 SCAN YOUR CALENDAR
Look back and forward two weeks
for anything that needs action.

3 CHECK ALL YOUR LISTS
Go through Action and Project lists.
Check done items.
Add new actions.
Chase "Waiting For" list if required.

4 GET PERSPECTIVE
Review goals and project plans.
Reflect on whether your life needs rebalancing.
What really matters?

Execute!

Once your mind is clear and your actions are clear, you
can do what needs to be done with a lot less friction. You
don't need to think twice. You just need to do. Although
it can take time to set up, once you have a system in place
your work, your mind and your breath will work a lot more
smoothly. In Chapter 6, "Focus," we will look at how you
can decide what to do more easily if things still aren't clear.

Tools of a Mindful Doer

By standardizing your favorite tools and equipment and making sure you always have re-stocks, you will always be ready to do. Here is my basic checklist:

AT MY DESK

— Notepad
— Great pens
— Index cards for
  brainstorming
— Filing cabinets
— Tabbed filing folders
— In-tray

OUT AND ABOUT

— Pocket notebook
— Zip folder

ON MY COMPUTER AND SMARTPHONE*

— Calendar
— Contacts
— To-do lists
— Documents in the Cloud
  (e.g., Dropbox)
— Notes
— Writing
— Password manager

*Note about apps:
I put all these everyday utilities in easy-to-reach places on my phone and computer like the home screen or dock and hide distracting ones away in folders.

Find tools you love to use and stick with them. For a list of the ones I like to use, please see the resources section at the end of the book.

By being very clear about what you use and why, you reduce mental friction and find more flow and joy in every task. Don't forget to breathe mindfully between tasks! Before switching apps or tasks, take a few breaths from the belly to stay calm and focused.

Exercise 1: Declutter your mind

Find a quiet spot where you can be alone for an hour or so. Make a nice cup of tea, grab a few cookies, put on some relaxing music, and get ready to clear your mind.

Use the lists below to trigger thoughts that are still lingering. Write down whatever arises, without judgment, using a small pad and one thought per page. Things to do, to buy, to fix, to arrange, to sort out, to plan, to cancel, and so on.

Once you have finished and your mind is clear you will probably feel (a) relieved that your mind is empty (for now!) and (b) a little overwhelmed that you have a lot more stuff to deal with than you thought.

Now put all those pages into your in-tray and sort through them one by one. Follow the flowcharts given earlier in the chapter, and where you find friction or the necessary tools insufficient, correct and improve where possible.

Only by bravely facing your life as it is can you start creating your life as it will be.

Mind Declutter – Trigger List
Here are some suggested lists to give you a starting point.

AT HOME

Family / Friends / Community / Events / Hobbies / Household / Health / Fitness / Creativity / Transportation / Clothes / Pets / Schools / Clubs / Administration / Technology / Storage / Holidays / Financial / Legal

AT WORK

Projects already started / Projects coming up / Innovation & research / Legal / Staff / Technology / Office / Sales & marketing / Business development / Networking / Training / Financial / Things to read / Meetings

Exercise 2: Declutter your space

Now for the physical clutter. Start with one place, maybe your office or desk. First, pick up objects one by one and ask yourself:

1. Have I used this in the last six months?
2. Do I love it?

If the answer to both of these is no, then recycle or dispose of the item.

Then with what's left, group similar things together:

1. Stationery
2. Reference material
3. In-tray for stuff to deal with
4. Inspirational stuff

"Have nothing in your house that is not fit for purpose or beautiful"

William Morris

Things to Remember

1. Write things down rather than holding them in your head.
2. Get the best organizational tools in place and stick to them (at least for a year!).
3. Make time every day to think through stuff and create your next actions.
4. Meet with yourself once a week.
5. Declutter your work space at least once a week.

The last great adventure is you.

—

Tracey Emin

Hopefully by now you are breathing better and are in the process of getting more organized, so why are you still feeling so unsure about yourself? If this is not you and you have no problem facing your fears, learning from your mistakes, and thriving on challenges, then please skip this chapter.

Good. I'm not alone then. The Greek philosopher Socrates said, "The unexamined life is not worth living," and he had a good point. The more you look inside openly and honestly, the more baggage from your past you find. Many stop at the first ugly suitcase; few empty the closet completely.

Over the next few pages I hope to share some of my own experiences in this process of self-inquiry. It's not psychotherapy but it might help unravel some stuff that's holding you back from being brilliant.

Don't Limit Yourself

"Focus on what you're good at and forget the rest." I'm not sure if this voice in my head was an actual memory or not . . . a teacher, my father, or maybe a boss early in my working life. But wherever it came from, it made an impression that took a long time to shift. The educational psychologist Carol Dweck talks about fixed and growth mindsets and how we can hold different ones in different areas of our lives. We might be open to the possibility of being able to create the "perfect" body through nutrition, working out, and the right trainer and yet closed to any possibility of actually writing a blog post that someone might want to read. How true are these beliefs? What negative beliefs do you have about yourself? Ask if they are really true. What self-imposed limits are stopping you in your tracks? Recognize your limits and start to question them.

Grow Your Mindset

Children very quickly fall into fixed mindsets that can prevent them from progressing. They can think that making an effort is an admission of a lack of talent.

However, their mindsets can be a better indicator of how well they do than their talents. Dweck introduced classes in primary schools that focused on shifting students' mindsets from "fixed" to "growth." She explained how the difficulties encountered when we struggle with something causes the brain to create new pathways. Finding something difficult is a good sign, as it encourages the brain to adjust and grow. Students were praised for effort rather than the end "correct" result and shown diagrams of how the brain works. Carol found that by changing pupils' mindsets, they started to improve dramatically in subjects that they had previously given up on.

Do you have a fixed mindset about something in your life? Can you turn an obstacle into a challenge? Do you want to go through life or *grow* through life?

Feel the Fear

Be honest. What do you do when you feel afraid? Eat cake? Buy sneakers? Have a drink? Go for a run? Most of the time we find fear so uncomfortable that its presence is often fleeting. We just can't bear it. We are in awe of others who seem to have transcended it. We fear the day it will return. We fear *fear*. We stop feeling and start internalizing, metaphorically hiding our demons in big black trash bags and stashing them in the basement of our mind.

This suppression of fear can manifest in a number of ways. For some there is a gradual buildup in physical tension, often in the neck and shoulders. For others there is a nervousness in the gut that can lead to irritable bowel syndrome. For many we just learn to live small and aim low in the hope that we will never feel that fear again. And yet we do. It's a part of life. So isn't it better to feel it in pursuit of something that matters to us and is worth feeling some discomfort for now and again?

The reason why Eleanor Roosevelt advised us to "Do one thing every day that scares you" is because that is how we learn to live with fear and work through it.

Expect Less. Assume Less.

Back in my advertising days, one of our clients was Ford. We launched the Ford Focus in Europe with the slogan "Expect more." Life coaches and managers are always suggesting we raise the bar. But for me the problem is not in the "more" but in the "expectation."

In yoga philosophy there is the concept of karma yoga— the yoga of action—where we act to the best of our ability without attachment to the outcome. This doesn't mean that you don't *have* any outcomes, goals or plans, but once you have them, you focus on what you can do now. Expectation is the breeding ground of discontentment; it can disturb your attention and be detrimental to your ability to act skillfully.

Another misconception that can lead us astray is assumption. Rather than admitting that sometimes we just don't know, we make assumptions. Sometimes we do it so well that we start to feel that these assumptions are truths. We react to them as if they were real. We become blind to the reality in front of us and bewildered by this stuff of our imagination. There is a place for imagination and creativity, but don't confuse it with your current reality. As the artist and designer James Victore quotes from the Talmud, "Teach your tongue to say 'I don't know.'"

Feeling uncomfortable with the facts is hard enough. Don't make it worse by feeling even more confused by your expectations and assumptions. It's better to stay with "not knowing" than creating "false knowing." By facing the unknown bravely, we discover new ways to learn.

Eat Frogs

One way of getting a little braver every day is to eat frogs. Not literally, although I do remember feeling very brave in my pre-veggie days eating frogs' legs on vacation in France once. Productivity writer Brian Tracy says to start each day by doing the single most important thing that you need to do but normally avoid because it scares you. He calls these difficult tasks "frogs," and in order to deal with them, you *have* to eat them. So how do we confront and deal with the things we avoid through procrastination?

1. **Breathe**: You can feel resistance and fear, so don't make it worse by allowing it to escalate into a full-blown stress attack. Keep breathing.

2. **Think**: Are there any practical things you need to do first? Or is the "frog" the next action?

3. **Act**: Even though there is an inner voice pleading with you to delay, start moving. Pick up the phone, start typing the email. As Canadian businesswoman and author Danielle LaPorte says, "Surprise your doubts with action."

Shrink 'n' Shift

Think big, start small. To get momentum, drive your big vision down into simple actions and do at least one small thing every day. To make changes, you need to move out of your comfort zone. It will be uncomfortable. But you will grow. And that will feel great.

Exercise 1: Create a personal paradigm shift

Sit and write down all the things you think about yourself that hold you back: limiting beliefs, fixed mindsets, assumptions. Spend at least ten minutes doing this. Be honest. Dig deep.

Now circle the two things that hold you back the most.

Can you paraphrase them now with a potent short sentence that will make them obsolete? For example:

"I'm not smart enough to do this."

Your Personal Paradigm Shift could be:

"I am far more intelligent than I think I am—and just as smart as anyone else who does this."

You will know you have found something powerful when it makes you feel slightly nauseated saying it. It will go against a loud inner voice that will desperately try to convince you to change it or tell you that you are wrong.

Exercise 2: Power pose

Your posture can change the way you feel about yourself. Lift up your chest now and drop your shoulders back. Do you feel more confident? More capable? Next time you feel you are lacking the confidence and power to do something, why not strike a "power pose?"

— Stand upright with your feet slightly wider than your hips and your hands placed on the hips.
— Take some slow deep breaths, starting in your belly and moving up to the top of your chest.
— Stay like this for one to two minutes.

Why not combine the two each morning as a way to supercharge your day?

Things to Remember

1. Don't limit yourself.
2. Get comfortable with being uncomfortable.
3. If you're avoiding a difficult task, "eat the frog" and deal with it first.
4. Repeat your Personal Paradigm Shift statement every day.
5. Strike a power pose.

And breathe...

PRACTICE

4
Mindfulness

Forever is composed of nows.

Emily Dickinson

All of your life happens in the present moment. As the father of the resurgence in modern-day mindfulness, Jon Kabat-Zinn, said: "The little things? The little moments? They aren't little." And yet how rarely are we living in the moment? As you read this, are you really here? Is your mind drifting back into the past? Or projecting into the future? Have you ever driven your car and wondered how you ever got to your destination safely as you were lost in your thoughts? Before you can be mindful, you need to accept how mindless you are most of the time. Sounds harsh, but it's true.

The Essence of Mindfulness

My approach to mindfulness is free from dogma and tradition. It is fueled by my own life and experience. It is not a belief system but an attempt to harness a natural human potential that has become overlooked, particularly in recent times. No one tradition can really "own" mindfulness and yet as its popularity (and commerciality) grows, there is a turf war for ownership. I advise you to follow your experience and not any one system (this one included!).

I introduce my six-week "Mindfulness Made Easy" course with the simple explanation that mindfulness is a blend of:

1. **Relaxed attention**
2. **Acceptance**

Relaxed attention

Paying attention sounds serious. Concentration involves effort. Focusing on one thing is hard. There is a good reason for adding the word "relaxed." For many this is confusing because they don't associate relaxation with attention. They might even find it paradoxical. And yet it is exactly this blend that creates presence.

Acceptance

One of the most distracting traits we have is our desire to want things to be different from the way they are. Somehow we believe that we can simply think things away. But we can't. As the serenity prayer repeated in Alcoholics Anonymous meetings says, "Grant me the serenity to accept the things I cannot change, the courage to change the things I can, and the wisdom to know the difference." Acceptance is not to be confused with putting up with stuff, though. Once you fully accept the reality in front of you, you can then choose how you respond. By accepting without judgment what "is," you can "be" there fully.

With attention and acceptance, you live more in the moment and less in your head. Now let's look at how we can bring this to our daily lives.

Breathe Mindfully

In Chapter 1, I outlined how to breathe well to reduce stress. Traditional mindfulness practices, however, focus on observing your breath as it is without trying to influence it in any way. Your breath is always with you— a constant companion—so as you notice it more, you can't help but be more present. It's like an antidote to being lost in your head. And it's fast-acting. As you read this now, how are you breathing? Where can you feel your breath? Can you just watch your breath without thinking about it? Can you just feel it coming and going? Can you count ten breaths, just feeling them without thinking?

1. Inhale . . . exhale
2. Inhale . . . exhale
3. Inhale . . . exhale

Mindfulness of your breath is a foundational practice to mindfulness meditation. Its simplicity should not undervalue its power to transform your awareness. By regularly bringing your attention to your breath, you are cultivating your inner mindfulness muscle, and who knows, one day maybe you will count one hundred mindful breaths without wandering off!

Reconnect to Your Senses

Every moment you are awake, your senses are on. As you become more aware of your senses, you notice how rarely you just sense rather than think about your senses. As your sensory awareness develops, your senses become more heightened. You notice more details and nuances, experiencing greater pleasure from subtler stimuli. You become a fascinated observer, without analyzing or judging your experience so much. Your senses bring you back to living in the moment, just like your breath does.

Here are some straightforward exercises to become more mindful of your senses:

Taste

Take a small piece of dried fruit. Observe the appearance, take a sniff—notice how saliva starts to form in the mouth. Place it on your tongue and close your mouth. Move it around your mouth without chewing. There are four basic types of receptors in the mouth to discern taste: sweetness, bitterness, sourness, and saltiness. Before chewing, what can you taste? Relate to the taste without naming it. Start to chew slowly. Notice the increase in saliva, the changing tastes and sensations. How do you feel? Do you feel emotionally different? As you swallow, be aware of the sensations in your throat and any other feelings in your body. Notice the aftertaste in your mouth.

Smell

Find somewhere that stimulates your sense of smell. Go outside or go to the kitchen or just start where you are now. I love the smell of new books, don't you? Do any smells evoke feelings of hunger, desire, or particular memories? Try smelling different things, removing any judgment from the experience (which is hard). Flowers, incense, soap, or perfume . . . food, spices or plants . . . your trash can, your pet's bed, your coat. Investigate the scents you find—both natural ones and artificial ones—without trying to label them. Smell for the sake of smelling. Breathe in deeply. See if you can identify any new smells.

Feel

Sit down in a chair, if you're not already in one. Feel the chair, the texture. Feel the weight of your body. Feel your feet, in your socks, in your shoes, on the carpet. Stand up and feel your feet firmly planted on the ground. Walk around and pick up a selection of objects with different textures—wool, cotton, nylon, wood, metal, plastic . . . Select items with different qualities—smooth, rough, wet, slimy, hot, or cold. Touch and feel each one without analyzing. Touch your skin. Give yourself a tickle (is it really impossible to tickle yourself?), a scratch, a rub, a tap on the leg. Use other parts of your body to touch things: your forearm, bare feet, your scalp.

Walk outside and feel a soft breeze against your skin. Half of our nerve endings are in our face, feet, and hands.

See

Take a walk on a familiar route. See what you can notice now that you are consciously bringing your awareness to it rather than being lost in thought. Choose a color. Look around you as you walk and see what things you can see in that color. Can you observe objects without immediately labeling them? Can you see a tree without thinking "tree"? Stand still for a moment. Without moving your head, become aware of your peripheral vision. How far to the right and left can you see? Look at something close to you. Observe it in even finer detail. (Put on your reading glasses if you wear them.) Now look into the distance and see how far you can see. Have you noticed anything new?

Listen

Just listen. What can you hear? Bring your awareness to sounds close to you. Maybe the ticking of a clock or your watch. Put your fingers gently in each ear and listen to the sounds within your body. Can you hear your breath? Your heart? Your stomach? Pick up a pen and tap objects to hear their sound. Notice the different tones that are generated. Bring your awareness further afield to sounds far away. Can you hear any traffic noise? Are they cars, trucks, or bikes? Maybe you can hear a TV next door or a distant washing machine. Maybe you can hear the sound of birds singing. Isolate one sound and focus on it. Be interested in the quality of it, the frequency, the feeling of it. What's the loudest sound you can hear? What's the quietest? Suspend any judgment about the sounds you hear. They are not good, or bad, they just are.

Find Time to Relax

There are many ways to relax, but unfortunately much of what we do to relax has the opposite effect. Think about what you do to relax at the end of a day at work. Most of us watch films, play games, or interact on social media, and in doing so, we continue to overstimulate our nervous system at the time when it desperately needs a rest. We drink alcohol and eat comfort food that puts pressure on a number of the body's internal systems. It's not surprising that so many of us sleep badly and arrive at work the next day feeling exhausted.

The truth is we are not very good at doing nothing. So can we get better at not doing?

First, we need to allocate time to relax, time to simply be. We can make a big difference in how we feel by doing one of the five-minute exercises below, which enable our bodies to enter a restorative state.

Second, we need to change what we do at work, at home, and when we're out and about so that we don't overstimulate ourselves so much. And for this, too, I will make some simple, practical suggestions.

Exercises: Five-minute relaxation

1. **Tense and release**
   Lie down somewhere warm and quiet. Move through your body from your toes to head, systematically tensing and then releasing all your muscles. Tense your toes . . . and release. Tense your legs ... and release. When you have completed tensing and releasing your entire body, just lie there with your eyes closed, following your breath.

2. **Auto-suggestion**
   Again lying down somewhere warm and quiet, close your eyes. Repeat to yourself silently: "My toes are relaxing, my toes are relaxed. My feet are relaxing, my feet are relaxed. My calves are relaxing, my calves are relaxed. My knees are relaxing, my knees are relaxed . . ." Make your way up your body, finishing with "My brain is relaxing, my brain is relaxed."

3. **Body trace**
   Lying down on your back, mentally trace a line around your body and observe how each part of your body feels as you go (without judgment). Start at the top of the head and work your way down your left side and then up your right side, finishing at the place you started.

Suggestions for more restorative downtime

— Replace TV time with reading time.
— Take a long, candlelit bath.
— Do some gentle stretches.
— Give yourself a massage or ask your partner to
  massage you.
— Take time to cook some healthy food and enjoy
  the process.

Maria Popova of BrainPickings.org refers to her moments of
calm as "pockets of stillness." What are your favorite ones?

Whatever You Do, Do It Mindfully

As you learn to be more relaxed and more present, you
will discover that even everyday actions can take on
another guise. As a Zen master once said, "When walking,
walk. When eating, eat." So tomorrow morning when you
brush your teeth, really brush them. Not differently, but
mindfully. Pay attention to the movement of your hand,
the toothbrush, and the toothpaste being squeezed on.
Notice the smell, notice the colors, notice the taste and the
sensations in and around your mouth. Be fully there.
If you drift into your thoughts, just keep coming back to
the feeling of brushing your teeth. Now think of three
other things that you can do mindfully today: Drink a glass
of water. Make a cup of tea. Water your plants. Drive your
car. Take a shower. Wash your dishes. Go running. This
shouldn't slow you down, but it might help calm you down.

Walk on by

Walking mindfully brings the benefits of mindfulness and exercise together in a simple daily activity. First, be aware of your feet on the ground before you start to move. Rock forward and backward, then side to side on the soles of your feet. Be aware of how your feet and toes feel. Walk in a straight line for a few steps, inhaling as you raise your right foot and exhaling as you plant it, heel first, then toes, then the same with your left foot. Next, inhale as you raise one foot and exhale as you raise the other. Walk up and down for a few steps, feeling your feet. Become aware of your body moving through space. Walk for ten minutes, dropping all thoughts of destination. Whenever your mind wanders, come back to the feeling of your feet, the movement of your body, and the sensations of your breath.

Don't just do something, sit there

Just sitting mindfully is sometimes called meditation. This often causes us problems, though, as the meaning of the word *meditation* and our assumptions and expectations around it ironically become barriers to us doing it. So don't think about it too much, just sit. On a chair, on a cushion, kneeling, or cross-legged. Sit upright with your chest up and shoulders back. Draw in your belly to support your lower back. Feel your breath. Feel your body. And practice the art of being present. Notice thoughts that arise like clouds on a blue sky. Acknowledge them, and then let them go. And if you don't, then just accept that, too. With time you will find less mental resistance and cultivate more patience. It's not easy but it is simple. Try spending five minutes a day just sitting every day for a week. Then add five minutes more until you can sit for twenty minutes each sitting. Think of it as mindfulness muscle building. You will be amazed by its effects.

Still Works

The name of my coaching and training business is Stillworks, and for nearly twenty years I have been personally amazed by the power of meditation, yoga, and mindfulness. In recent years, neuroscientists and researchers from around the world have discovered a number of important insights into the impact that meditation has on our physiology.

Through meditation, the brain experiences growth in areas associated with attention and processing of sensory input. Another unexpected research finding shows the expression of genes involved in immune function, energy metabolism, and insulin secretion are affected. Most recently, meditation has been shown to improve telomeres that affect ageing at the cellular level.

So as well as feeling better, thinking better, and enjoying life more, there's some very clever stuff going on inside your body, too, when you meditate.

Be still. It works.

Things to Remember

1. Make your breath your constant companion.
2. Reconnect with your senses.
3. Eat mindfully.
4. Walk mindfully.
5. "Just sit" once a day.
6. Listen more.

5
Energy

> The difference between one man and another
> is not mere ability . . . it is energy.
>
> ---
>
> Thomas Arnold

The world is having an energy crisis. We are running out of fossil fuels and all too slowly moving toward sustainable ones. And yet we tend to overlook our own personal energy crisis. We tell ourselves it's nothing that a bar of chocolate or a can of Red Bull can't sort out . . . or is it?

Is Your Life Sustainable?

You can have the best intentions, a marvelous mind, and excellent advice on what to do and even how to do it—and yet without the required energy, it will fall flat.

But what do I mean by energy? Is it the calories we consume through eating and drinking? Is it the energy we expend through physical exercise? Or thinking too hard? Or arguing? Can we replenish it by sleeping and resting? Is it a chemical thing or is it more subtle? Is it affected by our emotional state?

I think of "energy" as being all of the above: mental fuel to enable us to think; physical fuel to enable us to move; emotional fuel to motivate us. How we sleep, what we eat and drink, how we unwind, and how we feel all affect our energy levels.

To understand this better, let's look at what a lack of energy looks and feels like.

Do You Recognize Yourself in This Example?

Richard is a creative director at a London ad agency. He wakes up at 7 a.m. but doesn't actually get up until 7.30 a.m. This time is spent processing thoughts about the day ahead, the things he didn't do the day before, and how tired and achy he feels. "I'm exhausted," is his first thought of the day. When he finally gets up and takes a shower, he then can't decide what to wear. He ums and ahs, getting irritated that the shirt he finally settles on hasn't been washed and he's left a particular jacket at the office. By the time he makes it downstairs for breakfast, he is running out of time to catch his train. He grabs a breakfast bar and heads off to the station. His fifteen-minute walk is full of negative thoughts about the day ahead and he feels guilty that he left the house without saying a proper good-bye to his family.

On the train he reads the free newspaper and notices a competitor's ad, which is annoyingly good. He gets depressed by the state of the world in the news and even more so by the results of his football team. By the time his train arrives he's ready to turn around and head straight back to bed.

"I really can't be bothered" is the thought dominating his mind.

As soon as he arrives at his office, he checks his email and feels overwhelmed by the new demands piling up on top of the existing ones. He is then called into a meeting that lasts two hours and he only manages to stay alert by drinking three cappuccinos made on the swanky new office machine along with some rather tasty cookies.

By lunchtime he still hasn't actually managed to do any real work and feels so bad he decides to work through lunch. He stuffs a sandwich down while replying to emails and trying to think of ideas for his afternoon meeting—none of which really excite him.

I could go on . . . Richard is struggling. Maybe you are too? He is not managing his energy well and is feeling stressed and anxious as a result. At the end of the chapter I will propose an alternative day for Richard where he is looking after himself and his energy better.

What Gives You Energy?

The following five things are key to successfully maintaining your energy levels:

1. Sleep better.
2. Feed your mind.
3. Move more.
4. Stop more.
5. Be positive.

Let's look at each of these to see what we can do.

1. Sleep better

Are you one of the 70 percent of people who doesn't get enough sleep? We spend on average a third of our lives asleep, so isn't it worth getting better at it?

While we sleep, our body and mind do some pretty clever things. So clever, in fact, that the world's leading scientists still don't fully understand it. Let's see what we do know.

There are four distinct stages of sleep that the body cycles through roughly every ninety minutes.

1. Falling asleep
2. Light sleep
3. Slow-wave sleep
4. REM sleep

In general, there are four to six cycles of NREM (non-REM) sleep (the first three stages) per night, which are followed by intervals of REM sleep. Throughout your sleep the periods of NREM become shorter and the periods of REM become longer. On average you spend about 20 percent to 25 percent of the night in REM sleep, and there is research showing that a lack of this can result in depression.

And that's not the only problem that can arise from lack of sleep.

— **Effects on your brain:** Lack of sleep impairs your memory, makes you irritable, renders you unable to think well, and makes you more prone to depression.

— **Effects on your heart:** Lack of sleep lowers your heart-rate variability and increases risk of heart disease.

— **Effects on your body:** Lack of sleep makes your muscles react more slowly, affects your physical control and accuracy, causes aches, and makes you more likely to get type 2 diabetes.

We need roughly one hour of sleep for every two hours we are awake, although Cheri D. Mah, a researcher at the Stanford Sleep Disorders Clinic and Research Laboratory, found more was even better. She had members of the Stanford basketball team sleep for ten hours a night for six to seven weeks. According to a *New York Times* report, "They reported not just higher energy and improved mood, but faster sprint times and improved free-throw and three-point shooting accuracy."

So what prevents us from having a good night's sleep?

— **Noise:** Particularly in the early stages of sleep, any noise can wake us up. As we drift into light sleep, a part of the brain called the thalamus puts a block on our senses so we don't wake up so easily. If you live somewhere noisy, try earplugs.

— **Routine:** If you're a parent, you will know the importance of a bedtime routine: e.g., bath, brushing teeth, book, and then bed. Create your own routine and make it a habit—Chapter 8 might help here.

— **Light:** The main way our body clock keeps us in sync is light. Our eyes react to light and dark, even when they're closed. Make your bedroom as dark as possible or try a sleep mask.

— **Stimulants:** Drinks high in caffeine make it harder to fall asleep and can result in more light sleep and less deep sleep (good for a "caffeine nap" though—see next section!). Alcohol can make us snore more, which affects our breathing and quality of sleep.

— **Thinking:** Does lying there with thoughts going round in circles sound familiar? Learning to switch off by relaxing and letting go is essential to getting to sleep more easily. Hopefully as you breathe better and manage your life better, this will get easier. If your head won't stop thinking, try writing stuff down— I keep a pad and pen by my bed and always find that it helps me.

Even if you're getting enough sleep at night, it's common to feel sleepy between 1 and 3 p.m. Although in our culture there is usually no place for a full siesta, there is increasing evidence that napping is good for giving you an afternoon energy and productivity boost.

Power napping for ten to twenty minutes is refreshing, as you wake up before entering the deep sleep stage. Drinking coffee before you power nap means you will wake up at roughly the same time as the caffeine kicks in. This is a great trick if you find yourself on a long drive and need to recharge fast.

A longer nap of ninety minutes (one complete sleep cycle) is the ideal way to catch up on lost sleep, especially when taken after lunch.

If you've tried napping and find that you wake up feeling worse, you may need to adjust the time you spend, as outlined above. There's even an iPhone app called Power Nap that times your nap just right for your own sleep rhythms, from the makers of the popular Sleep Cycle app.

Salvador Dalí was obsessed with the creative potential of sleep. With a tin plate on the floor in front of him, he would drift off to sleep holding a spoon. As he fell asleep he would drop the spoon onto the plate, causing him to wake up buzzing with new ideas.

Here are some other famous nappers:

— Leonardo da Vinci took multiple naps a day and slept less at night.
— Thomas Edison was apparently embarrassed about his napping habit, but he still did it every day.
— Eleanor Roosevelt used to nap before speaking engagements to give herself an energy boost.
— John F. Kennedy had lunch in bed and then napped.
— John D. Rockefeller napped every afternoon in his office.
— Winston Churchill reckoned his afternoon nap helped him get twice as much done each day.

2. Feed your mind

While I'm not a nutritionist, I do find that this "Top Ten Brainfood" list from the BBC website is worth taking on board.

1. Whole grains
2. Oily fish/flax seeds
3. Blueberries
4. Tomatoes*
5. Certain B vitamins (B_6, B_{12}, and folic acid)
6. Black currants
7. Pumpkin seeds
8. Broccoli*
9. Sage (it does what it says!)
10. Nuts

Whole grains with a low-GI (glycaemic index), which release glucose slowly into the bloodstream, like whole-wheat bread, oats, brown rice, and brown pasta, give the brain a steady supply of energy through glucose. Essential fatty acids and vitamins are vital to healthy brain function. Research has shown that nutrients such as these can slow the aging of the brain, improve mental agility, and reduce memory loss.

So next time you're feeding your brain with reading and learning, don't forget a healthy brain snack too.

If you have trouble shifting from unhealthy snacks, why not try this? Researcher Brian Wansink found that "you are three times more likely to eat the first thing you see in your cupboard than the fifth thing you see." So put the healthy things close and the not-so-healthy ones at the back of the cupboard (or even back on the store shelf before you buy them).

* Learn how to grow your own vegetables in *Do Grow* by Alice Holden.

You wouldn't dream of keeping plants and not watering them, and yet you often fail to water yourself. As your body is made of 60 to 70 percent water, maybe it's time to look after your inner garden just as much. The Mayo Clinic recommends approximately 3 quarts (3 liters) for men and 2.3 quarts (2.2 liters) for women every day. Dehydration not only makes you thirsty, it also affects how you think. Drinking water can help you eat less and control your weight. Your blood and cells carry more oxygen when they are well hydrated, which means you have more energy. Your brain works better and your skin looks better.

Are you drinking enough water?

Power Drink recipe

The Power Drink was first introduced to me by Dr. S.K. Kamlesh, an Ayurvedic physician. He recommends having this nutritious drink for breakfast. The almonds are excellent for the brain. The dry fruits will provide you with plenty of energy to go through the morning. Soaking retains all their qualities while making them easily digestible.

Ingredients: 5 almonds, 1 big dry fig, 1 or 2 dates (Medjool if possible), a few nuts (e.g., cashews or pistachios), a few filaments of saffron, a few drops of rose water

Instructions: The night before, soak the almonds in one bowl and the rest of the ingredients in a separate bowl. In the morning peel the almonds—this will be made easier after the overnight soaking. Pit the dates and mix all the ingredients in the blender, adding the saffron, the soaking water, and extra water if needed to adjust the consistency (it should remain quite thick). Add a few drops of rose water before serving.

3. Move more

Many areas of the brain light up during and after exercise. It's not a coincidence that some of your best ideas come when you're on a run or cycling or taking a long walk.

"When we exercise, blood pressure and blood flow increase everywhere in the body, including the brain," Justin Rhodes, associate professor of psychology at the University of Illinois, writes in the journal *Scientific American*. "More blood means more energy and oxygen, which make our brain perform better."

In *On Form* by Jim Loehr and Tony Schwartz, they reveal that the Canada Life Assurance Company found that 63 percent of its participants in a fitness program reported being more physically relaxed, less tired, and more patient during the workday. Some 47 percent reported being more alert, having better rapport with supervisors and coworkers, and experiencing a higher level of enjoyment at work.

So don't get down, get moving. "You reduce the risk of getting depression when you exercise," as neuroscientist and researcher Maria Lindskog puts it.

Gretchen Reynolds—who writes on the *Well* blog for the *New York Times*—said in an interview with *Time* magazine: "The first twenty minutes of moving around provide most of the health benefits. Twenty minutes a day makes a truly profound difference in your health and dramatically reduces the risk of a whole host of diseases, particularly diabetes, heart disease, and dementia, as well as cancer." Whether you run, cycle, walk, do yoga, or whatever, remember that you don't need to spend hours for it to be effective. Making exercise a less daunting task means you are more likely to make it a habit.

Here are three ways to move more without much effort:

1. **Take the stairs**: Say good-bye to the elevator and the escalator.
2. **Walk more:** Why not have walking meetings?
3. **Stand up more:** Have you tried a standing desk?

4. Stop more

Sometimes the best way to move forward is to stop. Resting is the best way to recover your energy levels. Like our ninety-minute sleep cycles, we also have ninety-minute cycles in the day. If we don't rest every ninety minutes, our energy levels become depleted.

Stop working late

Arrive early. Leave on time. Stop being a martyr. Working late means you are sacrificing your best work for your worst. When my first child was born I started leaving work on time, and after a week everyone accepted it and nothing awful happened!

Stop the glorification of busy

Busy is bad for business. And the glorification of busy is bad for life. Busy can be a great way of appearing to be working when in fact you are just filling time. Your best ideas don't come when you're busy. Next time you're about to say, "I'm too busy" . . . stop . . . and take a deep breath. Often the feeling of busy is one of avoidance and a way to distract you from an uncomfortable feeling. Maybe you are busy avoiding the fact that you don't like what you're doing any more. When you find your true passion, you feel exhilarated when you have a lot to do—not "busy."

Stop talking

One of the best ways to waste your energy is to talk too much. On yoga retreats it is common to spend long periods in silence. As well as allowing you to go within, when you stop talking you also start to realize how often we say things just to fill uncomfortable social situations. Try saying a little less and meaning a lot more.

Stop thinking

We all have thousands of thoughts every day. How many can you remember? How many of them are habitual, useless, or even harmful?

As the Tibetan Buddhist Sogyal Rinpoche says, "The trouble with us is we have overindulged in thinking. The result is mental, even physical, illness. Many Tibetan doctors have remarked on the prevalence in the modern world of disorders due to disturbances to the prana or inner air, which are caused by too much agitation, worry, anxiety—and thinking—on top of the speed and aggression that dominate our lives. What we truly need is just peace. That is why we find that even to sit for a single moment, to breathe in and out and let the thoughts and emotions quietly settle, can make such a wonderful break." *

Unnecessary thoughts and words are like a dripping tap. The tap doesn't appear to be losing much water but after a day the floor is flooded, and after a day of too much thinking and talking we are often exhausted by it. Try moving your attention from your thoughts to your breath. Notice the pauses between your breaths. As your breath stills, so does the mind. Or if your thoughts are overpowering, try to notice the gaps between the thoughts and pay them a little more attention. Mind the gaps. That's where you'll always find some calm.

* Source: Sandra Pawula's blog *AlwaysWellWithin.com*

5. Be positive

Dr. Barbara Fredrickson says in her book *Positivity*, "Negativity breeds health-damaging negative emotions—like anger, contempt, and depression—that seep into your entire body. You can feel the simmering bitterness eating away at your stomach, raising your blood pressure, and turning your shoulder and neck muscles to stone."

A positivity ratio of three to one of positive emotions to negative ones appears to be a tipping point enabling people to achieve far beyond what they thought they could. Her list of positive emotions include **gratitude**, **serenity**, **interest**, **hope**, **pride**, **amusement,** and **inspiration**.

If you spend more time noticing and appreciating these emotions, you are more likely to maintain your energy levels. However, our brains are wired to absorb negative experiences more easily than positive ones. So to combat this "negative bias," neuropsychologist Rick Hanson recommends savoring these positive experiences for at least fifteen to twenty seconds for them to sink more into our memories.

Last, don't forget the power of music. Nothing can lift your mood faster than the right track—this book wouldn't be here without the Black Keys, Radiohead, Grizzly Bear, and the National (to keep me going), and Joan As Police Woman, Lou Rhodes, and Joni Mitchell (to keep me calm). What music helps to nourish and sustain you?

A Better Day?

Going back to the start of the chapter, let's see what Richard's day might look like if he followed some of this advice:

The alarm goes at 6.30 a.m., not 7 a.m. Richard gets up and heads straight for the shower. He puts on the clothes he laid out the night before and goes downstairs. After a mug of hot water with a slice of lemon to kick-start his digestive system, he sits down and breathes mindfully for five minutes to get centered. He has a healthy breakfast of oatmeal, sprinkled with nuts and seeds, and a mug of tea. He asks his wife and children about the day ahead. As he leaves the house he thinks, "How grateful I am."

On his walk to the train station he treads mindfully, noticing his steps and taking in all the sights, smells, and sounds around him. During his train journey he listens to a podcast of some of his favorite comedy and arrives at work early and in a good mood. He takes regular breaks through the morning to stretch, walk, breathe, and drink water. At lunchtime he goes outside for a mindful walk before stopping for a light lunch somewhere. Throughout the afternoon he takes five-minute breaks every hour to keep his energy levels up and keep his creativity flowing. He makes his last meeting of the day a walking meeting so he can discuss some tricky issues in a more convivial way.

He leaves work at 6 p.m. (If the agency want his best work, they know he needs to rest!) Again he avoids the newspaper on the train, this time reading a new niche magazine that was recommended. Arriving home at 7 p.m., he takes five minutes to unwind and de-stress in his bedroom before changing his clothes and spending time with his family over dinner.

After reading stories to his children before bed, he watches an episode of his favorite drama on Netflix with his wife.

To prepare for a good night's sleep, he takes a long, candle-lit bath and then reads in bed for a while before turning off the lights. He remembers something he feels thankful for and then breathes deeply to relax and sleep well.

Things to Remember

1. Sleep well.
2. Eat well.
3. Drink water regularly.
4. Exercise three times a week for as little as twenty minutes.
5. Rest more.
6. Look for the positive.

Breathing Exercise 1: *Kapalabhati*

Kapalabhati (literal meaning—"shining skull") are rhythmic exhalations with a pumping action that flush out your lungs of old air, stimulate the nervous system, and release tension.

Sit in a chair or cross-legged with your back straight. Take three deep in-and-out breaths to prepare. Then draw your tummy in sharply as you exhale. Repeat once a second so you get into a rhythm. Don't hold your breath. You will be inhaling in between exhalations but not consciously. Just focus on the sharp exhalations. If you find this difficult, try placing your hand on your tummy and press gently with each exhalation. It can take time for your stomach muscles to react quickly enough. This exercise is only possible after you have mastered the belly breathing exercise from Chapter 1.

Repeat with twenty pumps at first and then breathe deeply and hold your breath for thirty seconds if possible. This is one round. Repeat for three rounds. You can build up the repetitions from twenty to thirty to forty to sixty. You can also learn to retain your breath for longer, too. Don't be too competitive though. Slow steady progress is best.

Breathing Exercise 2: Sun salutations

Sun salutations use 95 percent of your muscles. When done as a flowing exercise with the breath, they are the perfect way to energize you.

One round of sun salutation consists of two sequences, the first leading with the right foot in positions 4 and 9, the second leading with the left. Keep your hands in one place from positions 3 to 10 and try to coordinate your movements with your breathing. Start by practicing four rounds and gradually build up to twelve rounds.

1. Stand erect with feet together and hands in the prayer position in front of your chest. Make sure your weight is evenly distributed. Exhale.

2. Inhaling, stretch your arms up and arch back from the waist, pushing the hips out, legs straight. Relax your neck.

3. Exhaling, fold forward, and press your palms down, fingertips in line with toes—bend your knees if necessary.

4. Inhaling, bring the left (or right) leg back and place the knee on the floor. Arch the back and look up, lifting your chin.

5. Retaining the breath, bring the other leg back and support your weight on hands and toes.

6. Exhaling, lower your knees, then your chest, and then your forehead, keeping your hips up and your toes curled under.

7. Inhaling, lower your hips, point your toes, and bend back. Keep your legs together and shoulders down. Look up and back.

8. Exhaling, curl your toes under, raise your hips, and pivot into an inverted "V" shape. Try to push your heels and head down and keep your shoulders back.

9. Inhaling, step forward and place the left (or right) foot between your hands. Rest the other knee on the floor and look up, as in position 4.

10. Exhaling, bring the other leg forward and bend down from the waist, keeping your palms as in position 3.

11. Inhaling, stretch your arms forward, then up and back over your head, and bend back slowly from the waist, as in position 2.

12. Exhaling, gently come back to an upright position and bring your arms down by your sides.

This was taught to me by the Sivananda International Yoga Vedanta Centers (which also kindly shared the sun salutation diagram)—you can access some excellent resources on yoga at Sivananda.org. There are also video demonstrations on DoBreathe.com.

6
Focus

Do what you can,
with what you have,
where you are.

———

Theodore Roosevelt

Now that we've become more mindful in our everyday and built up our energy reserves, let's look at what's getting your attention and where our breath can help us focus.

Often we think of focus as the ability to keep our attention on one thing. The real power of focus, though, comes when that one thing is aligned with a greater sense of direction and purpose. So when you focus on something, make sure it's the right thing. You don't want to climb a ladder only to find it's leaning against the wrong building.

When Paul McCartney was asked about his relationship with his wife Linda, he said, "I'm the wide-angle and she is the zoom." For me, "focus" is both the ability to zoom in on a particular task and also to take in the bigger picture at the same time. You could call this an informed focus, an intentional focus as opposed to an obsessional and narrow one. This negative side to focus—when we become obsessed with a video game, for example—is called hyper-focus. Let's see if you can develop a healthier focus.

What Do You Care About?

When the designer Frank Chimero was asked how he maintains focus (on work, dreams, goals, life), his answer was simple: "You do one thing at a time." On his *43 Folders* blog, Merlin Mann, writer, speaker, and star of my favorite podcast *Back to Work*, qualified this with what he called "Step Zero: First, care."

If you find yourself frequently distracted, maybe there's a good reason. Maybe you're not doing what you really want. So before you focus on anything, ask yourself: Do I even care about this?

One way of finding out how much you do care is to ask yourself, "What would I stop focusing on to do this?" Maybe to focus more you need to "unfocus" and let other things go. What would be on your "not to do" list?

As Mann says: "Own your distractions, resist fiddly half-measures, and never for a minute allow yourself to believe that productivity systems, space pens, or a writing app that plays new age music while you stare at a blank page in full-screen mode can ever teach you anything about how to care. That's all on you. So, first: Care. Then, as you'll happily and unavoidably discover, all that 'focus' business has a peculiar way of taking care of itself."

Let's be honest, though. Most of the time our minds are all over the place. And long ago, yogis knew all about that.

A Yogi State of Mind

The word *yoga* refers to both the goal (self-realization) and the means of getting there (the practices). According to *Patanjali's Yoga Sutras*, which is one of the key ancient texts, the goal of yoga is "the stilling of the mind": Y*ogash chitta vritti nirodhah.* On the way there he refers to the five states of the mind. Thousands of years later, I think we can still relate to them.

1. **Scattered** (*kshipta*): You feel disturbed, restless, and troubled. Your mind wanders constantly. This is the most uncomfortable state to be in.

2. **Dull** (*mudha*): You feel dull, heavy, depressed, and forgetful. You want to do nothing and feel really lazy.

3. **Distracted** (*vikshipta*): You can concentrate only for short periods of time. This is monkey mind or noisy mind. This is where we spend the most time.

4. **Focused** (*ekagrata*): Your mind is one-pointed, focused, concentrated. When the mind is in this state, internal and external activities are simply no longer a distraction. The mind is fully present in the moment.

5. **Mastered** (*nirodhah*): You have mastered your mind and found inner stillness. This is not dissimilar from the "flow" state discussed in the next chapter.

All the advice in this book is geared to moving you out of the first three states into the more focused and harmonious ones, with the tools you need to navigate that journey.

How Meditation Improves Focus

One of the fundamental exercises for improving your focus is meditation. The world-renowned neuroscientist Richard Davidson, of the University of Wisconsin–Madison, says there are two key scientific benefits to meditation practice:

1. It strengthens the brain's ability to move from one focus of attention to another.
2. It improves the brain's ability to resist distractions.

These are essential aspects of self-control and becoming more focused. At the end of this chapter is a simple breathing exercise that leads you into this more focused meditative state.

"If you just sit and observe, you will see how restless your mind is," Steve Jobs told his biographer, Walter Isaacson, "If you try to calm it, it only makes things worse, but over time it does calm, and when it does, there's room to hear more subtle things—that's when your intuition starts to blossom and you start to see things more clearly and be in the present more. Your mind just slows down, and you see a tremendous expanse in the moment. You see so much more than you could see before. It's a discipline; you have to practice it."

Personally I found a symbiotic relationship between being more organized and focused in my everyday life and my meditation practice. As I meditated more, my life became more organized, which in turn helped my meditation.

The film director Martin Scorsese has this to say about his meditation experience: "For the last few years, I've been practicing meditation. It's difficult to describe the effect it has had on my life. I can only mention maybe a few words: calm, clarity, a balance, and—at times—a recognition. It's made a difference."

Whether you like the idea of meditation or not, it certainly makes sense if you want to find focus and get stuff done.

Make It Harder or Make It Easier?

One of the best ways to reduce everyday distractions is to make it harder to do the things you shouldn't be spending energy on and easier to do things you want to focus on. In Chapter 2 I recommended switching off notifications on your phone and your computer; you could also bury distracting apps in folders. No more Pavlovian bells to whet your appetite for distraction. In Chapter 5 I mentioned putting unhealthy food at the back of the cupboard and healthier snacks at the front. To focus well, sometimes you need to block out as much as you can. Out of sight, out of reach—from your phone, your computer, your mind, and the place you're in. Send your brain a signal that it's time to focus by putting on your headphones and playing your favorite tunes for getting in the zone. (Unless you've mastered your meditation habit and have no more need for these life hacks.)

Don't Fritter Your Days Away

We are all guilty of wasting time, from wasting minutes to wasting hours and days. Are you wasting your time? Are you even aware of how you're currently spending it?

1. **Track your time**. For a couple of weeks note down in your diary every half an hour what you're doing. Start a daily journal. Be honest. It's the only way to discover the present reality of your life. I use the app RescueTime (Mac) to track how I spend my time on the laptop.

2. **Analyze it**. Create meaningful categories and add it all up. Be as specific or general as you feel necessary. It really depends on your work and what you do each day and what you want to change.

3. **Plan your new days**. Once you've fully digested your current reality, you can plan it better. There is no right or wrong way, other than what gets you closer to where you want to be.

Some Advice on How to Focus Better at Work

Dustin Moskovitz, cofounder of Facebook and cofounder and CEO of Asana, a team task-management application, clears his schedule every Wednesday so he can get some uninterrupted project time.

Square CEO and Twitter chairman Jack Dorsey keeps organized by assigning a different topic to each day of the week. Monday: management meetings; Tuesday: product development; Wednesday: marketing and communications; Thursday: developers and partnerships; Friday: company culture and vision.

Merlin Mann always takes calls on Thursdays so when he meets someone new he can always slot in a catch-up call with them.

Michael Acton Smith, founder of Mind Candy, had some great advice in his Do Lecture to counter a lack of focus at work, saying, "The main thing is to keep the main thing the main thing."

The artist James Victore, who designed the cover of this book, says, "Mornings are wiser than evenings." I agree! When I coach top executives, one of the most common pieces of advice I give is to keep mornings clear to think and work and not fill them with meetings.

The Pomodoro Technique

One of the most effective techniques for getting something done without distraction or interruption is the Pomodoro Technique. Devised in the 1980s by Francesco Cirillo, the technique enhances focus and concentration and reduces the anxiety of time by using the simple tomato-shaped Pomodoro ticking kitchen timer. Now, of course, it is available as an app—and one that I frequently use.

Each burst of work in the Pomodoro Technique can be split into five simple steps:

1. Choose a task to be accomplished.
2. Set the Pomodoro timer to twenty-five minutes.
3. Work on the task until the alarm goes off (the ticking sound becomes quite hypnotic—in a good way).
4. Take a short break (five minutes is OK).
5. Every three or four Pomodoros, take a longer break.

You could use this technique to make the most of your ninety-minute ultradian rhythm, which we look at in the next chapter.

Let Your Mind Go for a Wander

The wandering mind can, though, be just the place for finding new ways of thinking. Creativity thrives on the unexpected collisions of thoughts that happen when we least expect them. So while it's good to be focused when it comes to getting stuff done, don't be so controlled that you dismiss the importance of daydreaming. This is a more natural mental state, so you probably don't need any advice on how to do it. Just be aware of when you need space to be creative and when it's time to focus.

Do One Thing at a Time

"You can do anything, not everything," says David Allen, the author of the bestselling *Getting Things Done*. So don't multitask. It's not really multitasking anyway, just fast switching between tasks that can actually reduce productivity by 40 percent, according to research. Focus on one thing at a time. Finish it (or a predetermined chunk of it). But how do you decide which of your many tasks to do?

Ask yourself:

— What can I do where I am now?
— What can I do with the time available?
— What can I do with the energy I have at the moment?

And then, if you are able:

— What will get me closer to doing what I really care about? (Or maybe what your boss really cares about if you're working for someone else.)

Let's break that down a bit.

Where are you?

First, let's look at the context you're in, the place where you are—your home, your office, your car, shopping, going for a walk . . . Is there any point in worrying about what you can't do, with what you don't have, in a place that you aren't in? And yet how often do we sabotage a situation by doing this? If you can't focus on what you really want to do where you are, you need to change focus!

How much time do you have?

If you have only ten minutes, don't start that big idea now unless you can break it down into something that can be done first in ten minutes. Be realistic. Sometimes getting smaller, less important things done in small pockets of time can lift your mood and set you up to tackle bigger tasks later or the following morning. Remember our frog eating.

How much energy do you have?

The degree to which you can focus on a task at hand depends on the amount of energy—mental, physical, or emotional—required to complete it. If you're feeling low, look for low-hanging fruit: less-demanding actions that will at least give you some momentum and match your energy levels. And if you find yourself procrastinating on those higher-energy responsibilities, then look at your general energy levels (see Chapter 5).

What really matters to you?

When faced with a number of choices, if you are clear about your direction and what you really love to do, then the decision will be easy. If you stumble here, I recommend reading *Do Purpose* by David Hieatt.

> "The purpose of life is to live it, to taste experience to the utmost, to reach out eagerly and without fear for newer and richer experience."
>
> ---
>
> Eleanor Roosevelt

The real power of a focused action is when it is aligned with something greater than yourself.

Breathing Exercise: Counting your breaths

Most people struggle with meditation. They either try too hard or are disheartened by the scattered nature of their minds. This simple breathing exercise can help bring you into a meditative state more easily. At first you might find it difficult to stay with the numbers and not wander off. If you do, just guess where you last were and keep going. You are training your mind to focus. See if you can get closer to completing the exercise each time until you master it.

Find somewhere relatively quiet where you won't be disturbed for fifteen minutes. Sit with your back straight and your eyes closed.

There are four phases to this exercise:

— **Phase 1**
Count silently both your exhalations and inhalations starting from fifty:
Fifty as you exhale, forty-nine as you inhale, forty-eight as you exhale, forty-seven as you inhale . . . all the way to twenty.

— **Phase 2**
Continue to count silently but count only the exhalations and then observe the inhalations without counting:
Twenty as you exhale, observe as you inhale, nineteen as you exhale, observe as you inhale . . . all the way to zero.

— **Phase 3**
Just follow your exhalations and inhalations for a few minutes mindfully.

— **Phase 4**
Just sit with your breath without any conscious effort. Just be. This is meditation.

Things to remember

1. Meditate!
2. You will naturally focus more easily if you are doing something you genuinely care about.
3. Do one thing at a time.
4. Switch off regularly to allow yourself to daydream (Warning: This will probably happen while trying to do No. 1).

PERFORM

7
Flow

A living body is not a fixed thing but a
flowing event, like a flame or a whirlpool.

—

Alan Watts

When someone says, "Go with the flow," it can sound
a little defeatist. Just take it, accept it, don't resist the
inevitable. And yet when Mihály Csíkszentmihályi*
wrote about "flow" in the 1970s, he was referring to
an optimal state of high performance and definitely
not a place of just settling into something. A ten-year
McKinsey study, for example, found top executives are
five times more productive in flow.

One of the results of being in flow are what Abraham
Maslow called "peak experiences"—"rare, exciting, oceanic,
deeply moving, exhilarating, elevating experiences that
generate an advanced form of perceiving reality, and are
even mystic and magical in their effect."

Flow can relate to moments of presence, though, as
well as high performance. A sudden glimpse of feeling
at one with yourself and all around you. And then there
are Eastern concepts of the flow of the universe, and
physiologists work on the flowing nature of our physical
bodies. Have you ever been in flow? Maybe you have
without even realizing it.

* Pronounced *chick sent me high* according to Merlin Mann—Csíkszentmihályi
pops up a lot in this chapter, so you'd better get the hang of it now.

In general we are rarely in flow. When people are randomly sampled, they are either bored or stressed—out of the flow channel. Our workplaces are not conducive to the flow state. Constant interruptions, electronic or physical, make it even harder. James Slavet, a venture capitalist, said on Forbes.com: "Studies have shown that each time a flow state is disrupted it takes fifteen minutes to get back in flow, if you can get back at all."

In this chapter we'll look at both the psychology of flow—and the flow cycle—and the physiology of flow, when our breathing and heart rates are fully in sync, leading to a state of coherence, or what high performers call "the flow state."

The Psychology of Flow

Let's start by outlining how applied psychologists look at the concept of "flow."

The flow channel

Flow happens when you feel a sense of challenge and are stretched yet you have just about the right skills to handle it. If the challenge is too great, you get anxious. If the challenge is too small, you get bored. In practice this journey into flow is a meandering path between the two of these.

The conditions for flow

Online sites and games designers measure the success of their work by the amount of time they can keep people in flow. This can result in what is sometimes called "the dark side of flow," where the intention is purely commercial and not always in the best interests of the person being manipulated. This makes me feel uncomfortable and I hope you direct your flow toward more meaningful endeavors—the world needs you to.

Owen Schaffer, a student of Csíkszentmihályi, lists the conditions for this elusive state:

— Knowing what to do
— Knowing how to do it
— Knowing how well you are doing
— Knowing where to go (if navigation is involved)
— High perceived challenges
— High perceived skills
— Freedom from distractions

I am looking to evoke the flow state not only in my clients, but in myself as well. Not only am I looking to evoke the flow state in my clients, but in myself as well. It is also central to the way my breathing app, BreatheSync, works; more on that later.

The process of flow

Jamie Wheal, the executive director of the Flow Genome Project, outlines the four parts of the flow cycle in his 2013 TEDx talk:

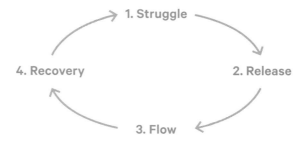

1. Struggle

Your journey into flow starts with struggle. You feel challenged but also stressed. Many give up here. It's why I wrote Chapter 3, "Courage." You need to dig deep. There is a risk of failure and you are feeling uncomfortable. If you can ride this out, you're on your way to flow. It is essential you have a growth mindset to see the obstacles as challenges to be overcome.

2. Release

This is where you let go and trust yourself. No mean feat. You have the skill, you just need to relax and allow yourself to do your best.

3. Flow

Aaah! You're in the zone.

4. Recovery

This can feel like a come-down. As I mentioned in previous chapters, you need to rest, you need to recharge. High-performance flow is transient. If you don't fully recover before going through this cycle again, you will not be able to handle the struggle at the start.

What does flow feel like?

"Flow" happens when a number of things come together at once:

— You feel fully present.
— Your being and doing are one.
— Your inner critic is asleep.
— You feel in control.
— You have lost a sense of time.
— You feel worthwhile.

If you've been following the exercises in previous chapters, you might have already had a "flow" experience. If not, you will soon!

Csíkszentmihályi calls the experience of flow "autotelic," explaining: "The key about an optimal experience is that it is an end in itself. The term *autotelic* comes from the Greek *auto* meaning 'self' and *telos* meaning 'goal.' It refers to a self-contained activity, one that is not done with the expectation of some future benefit, but simply because the doing itself is the reward." This is similar to the concept of karma yoga referred to on page 40.

Examples of people in flow

These examples are taken from Csíkszentmihályi's classic book *Flow*.

A dancer describes how it feels when a performance is going well: "Your concentration is complete. Your mind isn't wandering; you are totally involved in what you are doing . . . Your energy is flowing very smoothly. You feel relaxed, comfortable, and energetic."

A rock climber explains how it feels when he is scaling a mountain: "You are so involved in what you are doing [that] you aren't thinking of yourself as separate from the immediate activity . . . You don't see yourself as separate from what you are doing."

A mother who enjoys the time spent with her small daughter: "She reads to me, and I read to her, and that's a time when I sort of lose touch with the rest of the world, I'm totally absorbed in what I'm doing."

A chess player tells of playing in a tournament: "The concentration is like breathing—you never think of it. The roof could fall in and if it missed you, you would be unaware of it."

The Philosophy of Flow

The Eastern tradition of the Tao originated in China through the seminal book by Lao Tzu called *The Tao Te Ching*. It is difficult to translate the word *Tao*, although it is often referred to in the West as "The Way" or the "flow of the universe." In his Do Lecture in 2012, William Rosenzweig, co-author of *The Republic of Tea: How an Idea Becomes a Business* and founder of Physic Ventures, talks about "Wu Wei" as the art of non-doing. He quotes Lao Tzu—"Practice not-doing and everything will fall into place"—and goes on to explain the four ways of not-doing as:

1. Consciously not acting—being patient
2. Stillness—finding a place of quiet within
3. Effortlessness— the flow that comes from not trying
4. Doing without attachment to the outcome

It almost sounds like the complete opposite of the psychology of flow explained earlier in this chapter. And yet he is simply highlighting the phase before "Flow" in the flow cycle diagram, and the importance of "release" or "letting go."

For Rosenzweig there are five ways that he practices the art of "not-doing":

1. **Unplug:** Turn off the Internet and go off grid.
2. **Sit:** Just sit and be.
3. **Garden:** Nurture the earth.
4. **Listen**—mindfully.
5. **Give**—from your heart.

Flow leads us into what Rosenzweig calls the "magic, the mystery, and the meaning of life."

To do, you need to not-do. To give, you need to receive. To breathe in, you need to breathe out.

The Physiology of Flow

Picking up from research into sleep cycles (circadian rhythms), similar cycles (ultradian rhythms) have been observed in our workdays. Knowing when to do, and when to rest, can make a big difference not only to how you feel but also to how you perform. If you don't take breaks every ninety minutes, your productivity will decline. Ernest Rossi in his book *The 20 Minute Break* refers to these periods of rest as the "ultradian healing response."

Heart Rate Variability

One of the ways you can measure your energy throughout the day is by tracking your heart rate variability (HRV). This measure of heart activity is used in executive stress management, cardiology, and sports science and gives a good indication of your energy levels and vitality. Your heart has a rhythm—it's getting faster and slower all the time, even now. In fact, a healthy heart has high variability—a sign that your stress and relaxation responses are healthy. The dynamics of your heart enable you to cope efficiently with whatever life throws at you. If the variance is low, then you are either stressed, tired, or ill.

The first time HRV was used to monitor someone's stress was when the Russian space agency used it on Yuri Gagarin, the first man in space in 1961. HRV not only tells us whether you are stressed, it also impacts how your brain works and your life expectancy. It is also used to monitor any stress babies are under during childbirth.

Coherence

When your breathing rhythm is in sync with your heart rhythm, you are in what is called a *state of coherence*. According to Dr. Alan Watkins, "Coherence is, in essence, the biological underpinning of what elite performers call 'the flow state': a state of maximum efficiency and super-effectiveness where body and mind are one."

This state arises following periods of smooth and rhythmic breathing called *coherent breathing*. You can see the benefits of coherent breathing in the chart here.

	Shallow, irregular breathing	Coherent breathing
Body	Uncomfortable	Comfortable
Mind	Anxious	Calm
Muscles	Tensed	Relaxed
Blood flow	Decreased	Increased
Learning	Difficult	Natural
Sleep	Troubled	Restful

BreatheSync

Up until recently the technology to train people in these techniques has been expensive and only known by a few specialists. BreatheSync, the iPhone app that I co-created with my old school friend Simon Wegerif (who just happens to one of the world's leading experts on HRV), is designed to bring this to everyone who needs it.

BreatheSync works by utilizing the iPhone camera to measure a person's heart rhythm, and then creates a personalized breathing rhythm to center and relax the user, aligning with their individual heart-rate variability.

When you wake up, a one-minute check-in will give you your Wellbeing Quotient (WQ), which gives you a guide to your present physiological state. A two-minute BreatheSync can help center and focus the body and mind, reducing stress levels, and a three-minute or longer session will induce a state of deep relaxation.

People use it to prepare mentally for meetings, unwind at the end of a busy day, lower their blood pressure, and sleep better. Let me know if it works for you.

Yoga and Flow

We've discussed option to get in the flow using new technology, but yoga and meditation can also lead our bodies to this state of coherence. As Csíkszentmihályi (can you say it yet?) says, "The similarities between yoga and flow are extremely strong; in fact, it makes sense to think of yoga as a very thoroughly planned flow activity. Both try to achieve a joyous, self-forgetful involvement through concentration, which in turn is made possible by a discipline of the body."

Breathing Exercise 1: Coherent breathing

Use BreatheSync on your iPhone. Alternatively, breathe for five minutes or more with a smooth, steady rhythm (in for the count of five and out for five should be comfortable).

Breathing Exercise 2: Alternate nostril breathing

Your HRV is particularly improved by a technique called alternate nostril breathing. It helps create a focused, calm flow state by balancing your autonomic nervous system. Breathing through your right nostril is connected to your sympathetic response (fight or flight—the stress response) and your left nostril is connected to your parasympathetic response (rest and digest—the relaxation response). Most of us have overly active sympathetic branches of our nervous system, so this is a great way to regain balance.

Sit with your back straight. Close your right nostril with your right thumb and exhale through the left nostril. Inhale through the left nostril, close it with your right ring finger, and exhale through the right. Inhale through the right nostril, close it with your thumb, and exhale through the left.

And repeat.

Try to do this for three minutes, counting to three with each breath. In time increase the count to five. Six breath cycles per minute is for most people an optimum rate to affect your physiology.

Things to Remember

1. Set yourself challenges.
2. Be prepared for an initial struggle.
3. Do your most important work when you are in flow.
4. Don't forget the importance of regular breaks.
5. Breathe yourself into flow.

8
Habits

You are what your deep, driving desire is.
As your desire is, so is your will.
As your will is, so is your deed.
As your deed is, so is your destiny.

—

*The Brihadaranyaka Upanishad**

We are all creatures of habit. In 2006 a researcher at Duke University found that more than 40 percent of people's actions every day weren't actual decisions but habitual responses. Knowing this can make you feel powerless unless you believe in your ability to change those habits. Knowing which habits serve you and which ones don't is the first step in deciding where to start.

As a recovering alcoholic I guess I should understand this better than many. And yet although I have managed to change this significant habit for over twenty years (at the time of going to print I hope this is still true!), I still find it hard to create simple new habits. Don't we all?

You won't have reached this point in the book without really wanting to change or improve something in your life. Maybe it's how you manage stress, organize your stuff, feel more motivated, or breathe. Maybe it's all of them! One of my key aims is for us all to cultivate better breathing habits as a foundation for many others. So how do we kick bad habits and create long-term good habits in their place?

* Translated by Eknath Easwaran

Save Your Mental Capacity

Your ability to make decisions, focus, and understand is limited by your mental capacity. One of the easiest ways to manage your limited mental capacity is to turn everyday actions into habits: what you eat for breakfast, what you wear, and how you get to work. If you have to make decisions about these things every day, you can waste that mental energy. If they become habits, you can save that mental energy for more important matters.

Every morning, Steve Jobs would pick a black turtleneck from the top of a pile of black turtlenecks. As a habit, this required no mental effort. Apparently Barack Obama has a similar morning ritual, though a different style.

What everyday things could you turn into a simple routine to save energy and mental capacity?

Old habits create inertia—a sometimes impenetrable wall that can stop you in your tracks. New habits create momentum—the power to change, one thing at a time. But whether you are looking to change bad habits or start new, improved ones, first you need to understand what's really going on. You are going to need mindfulness, focus, and energy to do that. And at least a basic understanding of how habits work. Luckily, the mechanics of habits have been deconstructed for us.

The habit loop

There are basically three steps in what Charles Duhigg, author of *The Power of Habit*, calls "the habit loop:"

1. **Cue:** a trigger that tells your brain to go into habit mode and which habit to choose
2. **Routine:** a mental, physical, or emotional routine
3. **Reward:** the satisfaction you get as a result

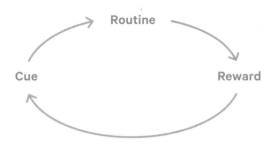

Routine

Cue

Reward

You can't always change the triggers or the rewards, but you can change the routines in between.

Duhigg gives his own example of going to get a cookie from the cafeteria at 3 p.m. every day, and putting on weight as a result. After some experimenting, he realized that the reward wasn't the cookie itself—it was the need for some social interaction, triggered by working on his own for too long. So he changed his routine and started having chats with colleagues whenever the cue (loneliness or boredom) happened, and lost weight as a result.

Can you think of negative routines that you have made into habits? Can you imagine replacing them with positive ones?

Once a routine has been done a few times, the brain decides to save energy by running it on automatic (which is what a habit is). This is why we can drive our cars from one place to another while thinking about myriad other stuff, arriving somewhat amazed that a subconscious part of us has been driving the car.

How Do We Change Negative Habits?

Identify the urge! Experiments have shown that almost all habitual cues fit into one of five categories: location, time, emotional state, other people, or immediately preceding action.

So, if you're trying to figure out the cue for the "going to the cafeteria and buying a chocolate chip cookie" habit, or whatever habit you're looking at, write down five things the moment the urge hits:

— Where are you?
— What time is it?
— What's your emotional state?
— Who else is around?
— What action preceded the urge?

These triggers can be either external or internal. External triggers include email and phone notifications; internal ones include the need for social interaction or to avoid uncomfortable feelings. Getting to the bottom of what actually triggers a habit is not always clear. You will need to ask yourself these questions a number of times before you get the right answer.

Can you identify a trigger for one of your bad habits?

The Root Cause

In his book *Hooked*, Nir Eyal suggests using the popular management consultancy approach of the "Five Whys" to get to the root cause. Taiichi Ono, of Toyota, one of the pioneers of this approach, explains the concept as "asking yourself 'why' five times until the nature of the problem as well as its solution becomes clear."

For example, do you really understand what makes you angry at work?

— *Why are you angry?* Because the project failed.
— *Why did the project fail?* Because it wasn't planned well.
— *Why wasn't it planned well?* Because I'm overloaded and stressed.
— *Why are you stressed?* Because I overreact.
— *Why do you overreact?* Because I don't control my breathing well.

So rather than venting your anger at the failed project or the bad planning, how about thinking about how your breathing affects the way you react?

Lack of effective stress-management techniques is the root of many problems at work today. And breathing well is at the root of stress management.

Through increased awareness of what is really going on, you can more effectively introduce positive routines that will cut your old habits down to size.

From Reaction to Response

Mindfulness creates space, a bubble of calm, between the trigger and the habit so you at least have a chance to change.

Through increased awareness of what is going on, you can respond more effectively and create new habits.

"Between stimulus and response there is a space. In that space is our power to choose our response."

Viktor Frankl

Without Mindfulness	Cue	Reaction		Old Habit

With Mindfulness	Cue	**Mindfulness**	**Response**	New Habit

Making New Habits Stick

The same thinking can be used to start a new habit too.

1. **Use existing habits as triggers**. You always put your keys and wallet in the same place. You always turn the radio on when you get in your car. You always brush your teeth before bed. Use these existing habits as triggers and link new ones to them.

2. **Make it easy**. If you want to meditate every morning, set up your meditation place the night before. Cushion, candle, matches, a blanket, the clothes you'll wear . . . If you want to take a bottle of water to work every morning, leave one by the front door before bed.

3. **Make a commitment**. Write down your goal for the new habit. Really commit. Reflect on why you want to do it. Reflect on the rewards you hope to get. Know your why!

4. **Tell a friend**. By sharing your intention publicly, you increase your chance of success.

5. **Create new triggers**. Leave sticky notes in all the right places. It may be time to turn back on some notifications on your phone, at least for a short period while you kick the habit. I use a habit- and goal-supporting app on mine (Coach.me).

A Cornerstone Habit

Certain habits can be thought of as cornerstone habits. They create a chain of consequential habits. Breathing well is the most important cornerstone habit you can have. For example: You feel stressed out and decide to regain control through breathing well. You feel better, so you empty your email inbox. This in turn creates a sense of control, which leads to you making a list of important tasks. Your confident state leads you to have that difficult conversation. Your sense of accomplishment leads to having a break and rewarding yourself with a walk in the park.

So just as breathing badly is the root cause of many other problems, breathing well can be the start of a positive chain of events.

Try implementing these breathing techniques so they become new habits:

Trigger	Old routine	New routine	Reward
Anxiety	Shallow chest breathing	Belly breathing	Calm
Worry	Sighing	Nostril breathing	Sense of control
Unexpected event	Holding breath	Exhaling to de-stress	Relaxed
Can't sleep	Get the laptop out	Slow, deep breathing	Sleep
Too much to do	Panic	10 mindful breaths	Renewed focus
Thinking too much	Going round in circles	Count your breaths	Clarity
Lack of energy	Cake!	*Kapalabhati*	Energy bost
Exhausted	Coffee	Full, deep breath	Momentum
Losing concentration	Keep switching tasks	Alternate nostril breathing	Centered
Nervous before meeting	Fret	BreatheSync	In the zone

Get into the Habit of Breathing Well!

— Before every phone call, breathe mindfully.
— Before you brush your teeth, breathe mindfully.
— Before you eat, breathe mindfully.
— Before you sleep, breathe mindfully.
— Before you drive, breathe mindfully.
— Before you write, breathe mindfully.

Continue the list yourself . . .

Exercise: Make a list of new habits you want to create

Spend some time reflecting on the previous chapters. Does anything jump out? Is there a particular issue you're struggling with?

Alongside each chapter title, write one simple new habit you would like to form. Then number them in order and start with the first one. Once the first habit is embedded (some say twenty-one days, some say longer), start the next one. Remember, the more good habits you form, the more mental energy you will have for the next one.

Things to Remember

1. Notice your triggers.
2. Change the routines around negative habits.
3. Cultivate new positive habits.
4. Take baby steps.

9
Well-Doing

To know even one life has breathed
easier because you have lived.
This is to have succeeded.

Ralph Waldo Emerson

**When I first left the world of advertising to become a
yoga teacher, I believed in the phrase "We are human
beings, *not* human doings." In my new life, I was
surrounded by people who believed in the power of
now and the importance of well-being, and "doing" had
a bad name. As I felt the first rumblings of desire to do
and create more, I felt confused. How could I do more,
without compromising my well-being?**

Over the last few years, as I have explored this inner
conflict, I have come to realize that this battle is waged
in the outside world too. It can appear as if there are two
tribes: the *beings* who believe life is about who you are and
how you feel, and the *doers* who believe life is about what
you do and achieve.

Now I realize that they are the two sides of the same
coin. There is *being* in *doing* and *doing* in *being*. In 2011,
I called this integrated approach to life *well-doing*. It is at the
heart of my personal life, my working life, and this book!

We are human beings *and* human doers.

Well-doing is not about balance—this assumes there
is an ideal state of balance when in fact life is myriad
moments in constant flux. *Well-doing* is about dynamic

balance—the ability to ride the waves of life with skill and joy. The same subtle but important shift in understanding has happened in the world of medicine too. The concept of "homeostasis"—when the body naturally looks for a state of balance—has been replaced by "allostasis," meaning a state of dynamic balance. This is explained in Robert Sapolsky's classic book on stress, *Why Zebras Don't Get Ulcers*, as being about "constancy through change."

At night, by allowing the mind and body to follow a natural rhythm of light and deep sleep, we are recharged by dynamic balance.

During the day, by following periods of effort with ones of rest, we maintain higher energy levels through dynamic balance.

With every breath we take, by creating a smooth, regular, and constant rhythm with our in and out breaths, we feel centered by dynamic balance.

Looking back at my life, there were a number of clues to these insights that I missed at the time but have discovered in researching this book. In a period of depression following the death of my brother, leading up to the new millennium in 1999, I was handed the book *You Can't Afford the Luxury of a Negative Thought* by John-Roger and Peter McWilliams. One of the chapters was about *being* and *doing* and the importance of both. I just wasn't ready to understand its significance back then, even if the authors admitted to including "jokes stolen from coffee mugs" to make their point:

Some say, "To do is to be."
Others say, "To be is to do."
I tend to agree with Francis Albert Sinatra:
"Do, be, do, be, do."

Later on, when I first picked up David Allen's *Getting Things Done*, which has been a major influence on how I get stuff done, I noticed it was dedicated to his spiritual coach J.R.—John-Roger, the co-author of *You Can't Afford the Luxury of a Negative Thought.*

So these worlds of being and doing merged—and that's where the magic is, and where this book was born.

The most technologically advanced machine known is our own "bodymind." By harnessing the human body's natural mechanisms, we have a built-in ability to manage stress. Simply breathing well and in sync with your body's natural flow creates the foundation for you to reach your full potential. By organizing yourself better and finding the courage to live outside of your comfort zone, you are transformed from "worrier to warrior," as James Victore would say. Practicing a more mindful life, you can appreciate the little things of life and savor the moment more.

Every breath is a wave. Every heartbeat is a wave.
Every thought is a wave. Every one of us is a wave.

All the waves that rise and fall exist on the vast ocean of our lives. Yet at the same time, mindfulness and meditation take us down into the depths of that ocean. To a place of stillness, peace, and inner calm.

Our doing and our being as one.

Well-doing is the synthesis of these contrasting experiences of life into one big dynamic whole. Embracing all that we experience and all that we offer with courage, skill, and love.

To find inner calm and outer focus we all need to embrace a range of strategies and techniques that bring together how we are with what we do. Reducing your stress levels, improving your energy levels, focusing your mind and attention on what really matters to you: These can transform your life. By playing with these ideas and integrating them into your daily life, I hope you, too, can find some magic and the passion to make it happen.

> "Working hard for something we don't care about is called stress. Working hard for something we love is called passion."
>
> Simon Sinek

There is an exercise that I once did inside a Tibetan Buddhist temple, not in some remote Himalayan village but in a terraced house in Seven Sisters called Jamyang. (It's moved now, I think.) Outside, the house looked perfectly normal. Inside it was a multicolored traditional Tibetan temple. We breathed in all the problems of the world and then breathed out loving kindness. Using this idea, perhaps you could join me in this last exercise that encapsulates the essence of all the chapters in *Do Breathe*.

— Breathing in . . . repeat silently, "*I am aware*"

— Breathing out . . . repeat silently, "*I accept*"

— Breathing in . . . repeat silently, "*I am calm*"

— Breathing out . . . repeat silently, "*I let go*"

— Breathing in . . . repeat silently, "*I am focused*"

— Breathing out . . . repeat silently, "*I feel relaxed*"

— Breathing in . . . repeat silently, "*I feel energized*"

— Breathing out . . . repeat silently, "*I am still*"

Notice the stillness inside as your breath flows through you. The word *inspiration* comes from the Latin word for "breath," *spiro*. I hope that this book has inspired you to breathe yourself better.

Breathe well. Be well. Do well.

One last thing: Please teach one other person you know to breathe well. It may change their life too.

———

Enjoy what is before it isn't.

Faustomaria Dorelli

Breathe out...

Resources

Visit *DoBreathe.com*, where you can watch videos and listen to audio of some of the exercises in the book as well as get links to all the resources below.

Books

Stress:
Why Zebras Don't Get Ulcers by Robert Sapolsky
Energy:
On Form by Jim Loehr & Tony Schwartz
The 20 Minute Break by Ernest Lawrence Rossi
The Relaxation Response by Herbert Benson
Positivity by Dr. Barbara L. Fredrickson
Flow:
Coherence by Dr. Alan Watkins
Flow by Mihály Csíkszentmihályi
The Tao Te Ching by Lao Tzu
Habits:
The Power of Habit by Charles Duhigg
Hooked by Nir Eyal
Organize:
Getting Things Done by David Allen
Mindfulness:
Full Catastrophe Living by Jon Kabat-Zinn
Zen Mind, Beginner's Mind by Shunryu Suzuki
The Power of Now by Eckhart Tolle
Yoga:
The New Book of Yoga by Sivananda Yoga Vedanta Centre
Life:
You Can't Afford the Luxury of a Negative Thought
    by John-Roger and Peter McWilliams
Meditations by Marcus Aurelius

Apps to Do

To Do: Things, Clear
Contacts: FullContact
Calendar: Fantastical,
Calendars 5
Notes: Drafts 4, Evernote
Documents: Dropbox
Habits: Coach.me, Balanced
Focus: Pomodoro
Time: RescueTime (Mac)
Steps: Moves

Apps To Be

Relax & Focus: BreatheSync
Sleep: Sleep Cycle
Nap: Power Nap
Mindfulness: BreatheSync,
Buddhify, Calm, Headspace

Podcasts

Work: *Back to Work*
Mind: *The Web Psychologist*
Body: *YOGAmazing*

Online Inspiration

James Victore
jamesvictore.com
Leo Babauta
zenhabits.net
Maria Popova
brainpickings.org
Merlin Mann
43folders.com
Seth Godin
sethgodin.com
Do Lectures
thedolectures.com

Audio & Video

For audio downloads and
videos of the following,
please visit DoBreathe.com

Audio:
Belly Breathing
Alternate Nostril Breathing
Full Yogic Breath
Kapalabhati

Video:
Sun Salutations
Breathe Yourself Better
BreatheSync demo

To share your experiences
on Twitter and Instagram,
please use *#dobreathe*

About the Author

Michael Townsend Williams is a doer who likes to be. From a life of "doing" in the world of advertising to a life of "being" as a yoga and mindfulness teacher, Michael now works on the integration of both. His business, Stillworks, coaches individuals, teams, and organizations on mindful productivity and mindfulness. He is also cocreator of the iPhone app BreatheSync, which brings your breathing into sync with your heart to reduce stress and improve focus. He believes the world needs to calm down and we would all get a lot more done if we did.

@mtownsendw | stillworks.org | breathesync.com

Thanks

Moira, my writer/producer wife, for her support and
inspiration; Dylan and Chloe, my children, for being
who they are; Betty and Ray Williams, my mum and
dad, for making me who I am; Jane Bates, my sister, for
her support and my London base; Faustomaria Dorelli,
my yoga teacher; Paul Thorpe-Tracey, my friend and
mentor; Miranda West, my editor and publisher; Clare
and David Hieatt, my inspiration to do as well as be; Ian
Sanders, my writing coach; Simon Wegerif, co-creator of
BreatheSync; Stephanie Weissman, founder of Inside Out
(theinsideout.org.uk); Swami Kailasananda, International
Sivananda Yoga Vedanta Center; Charlotta Martinus,
founder of Teen Yoga and Universal Yoga; Chantal de
Gaudio, artist and coach; Tim Drake, mentor; Ed Haddon,
coach and entrepreneur; Barry Walsh, coach; Mark
Lawrence, my first coach; Anne Scoular and Daniel Burke,
my train companions and coaches: James Victore
for his cover design, lettering, and general magnificence;
Wilf Whitty for making the book look great; Jonathan
Cherry and Mickey Smith for their stunning photos.
All my yoga and coaching clients, friends and supporters,
and BreatheSyncers around the world.

Index